A Box
of Darkness

A Poetry collection

by
Vivienne Tuffnell

For Kate Price,
in token of thanks for all the wonderful things
you do, for me and for others

A Box of Darkness

Contents

A box of darkness

You gave to me a box,
Hewn from a cedar heart
Carved and gilded
Buffed to a soft sheen
By mystery and curiosity
And the promise of within.
It held, you said, everything;
No less than that.
Don't open it yet, you said.
Wait till I am gone.
It holds all you need
To understand me.
The truth is, it did.
The box was empty;
It held only darkness,
And stale air, unbreathed.

23.7.2012

Inspired by some lines from the poet Mary Oliver

Accident of Birth

I was born a blonde
But beneath layers of fairness
There lurks a redhead,
Fiery, impulsive and hot.
I was born a Pisces,
On the cusp of Aries, Scorpio rising.
But I'm no bland cod-fish though:
I'm Jambalaya, in Cajun sauce.
I was born in the South;
Accident of fate, Northern stock.
Lose a leg? Hop, girl, hop!
They breed 'em tough up there.
I was born a woman.
But my inner man sits firm,
Fists balled primevally
Nursing a proper pint.
I was born complicated:
Don't try to understand me,
It'll just make your brain spin.
Best just let me be.

Berserker

Inside I am a warrior
But stripped of all armour
Naked but for the blood
That paints my trembling skin.
The axe I wield with one hand
A sword in the other,
Both held high.
The red mist waits,
Patient as a stone.
All you see is a woman
Middle-age spread
Greying hairs
Sagging breasts,
Virtually invisible, worthless.
But inside I am a warrior,
Waiting.
Don't push me.
You won't like the bear.

Black Dog

Hunt me down then,
Stalk me, track me,
Pin me down and corner me,
Pursue and torment me.
I'll fear your shadow
Even in noonday sun;
Scrape of claw on stone,
Foetid breath, panting tongue.
The silent nights
When I wait to hear
The footsteps on the stair,
And know you're there.
Black dog, you worry me.

Dog Days

Where did my summer go?
Lost in a whirl of passing days
Eaten up by anxiety
Consumed by confusion?
Summer ends as it began, silently,
Slowly, the greens fading
From brilliance to buff
Becoming at first tired and jaded,
Ragged at the edges,
The freshness of spring
Dried and hardened to leather.
The sun changes from the silver-gilt
Shining of May-time joy
To a brassy, aching shade
That burns and wearies the eyes.
Fermenting windfalls draw the wasps
Who feast amid drunken butterflies
Gorging themselves on over-ripe pears
And cider-smelling apples.
The harvest is all done;
Rough with stubble, empty fields
Await the blade of the plough
And the screaming gulls.

Breathe

I can't breathe.
Oh, my lungs work fine.
Watch: in, out, in, out.
But I still can't breathe.
I dream of mountaintops,
With air thin enough
To draw deep like wine,
Cold and sharp inside me.
I stand so high
I cannot see the ground.
I spread my wings,
Step forward, feel the rush
As I plummet, plunge and fall.
And then my wings support me;
I soar above the clouds,
The land below forgotten,
And just breathe.

Dangerous Age

I'm at a dangerous age:
Too old to be young,
Too young to be old.
Women like me straddle extremes,
A foot planted squarely on each.
I might do anything:
Run away to Bali,
Find adventure or a vocation,
Or stay home, learn bridge
And buy a shopping trolley.
I'm not done being young yet;
I'm not ready to exchange
My running shoes for slippers,
I'm not ready to cut my hair,
Colour away the silver threads
And save up for Botox.
I'm at a dangerous age:
Are you ready for this?

Beachcomber

The shores of sleep last night
Were not of soft white sand,
Strewn with intriguing driftwood,
Magical wave-smoothed rocks
And shining wine-coloured weed
Cast up from the deep.
No. The shores of sleep last night
Were strewn for miles
With the wrecks of dreams,
The hulks of hope
And fragments of fantasies,
Lying like beached and decaying whales.
Some looked whole and entire
Till I peered through portholes
And found them empty, no more than shells.
I would be a beachcomber,
Gathering material for my work
As I patrol this shoreline,
But I cannot work with this.
I will wait till the next storm
Washes the strand clean
Of cast-up wreckage
And leaves me with the flotsam
I can fashion and transform.

Burning

Shall I burn brightly:
The flight of a sparrow through
The fire-lit glory of the mead-halls
from darkness to darkness
With that brief passage
of brilliant light and heat?
Or shall I burn soft and subdued,
the banked peat fire through
long winter night of huddled homes,
Giving only a little but for long time,
Staving off freezing snows
with meagre, measured warmth?
Shall my show be the splendour
Of the fireworks at New Year,
Shooting flames and colour
High into the midnight sky?
Or shall it be the dim glow
Of the dark lantern,
Concealed and saved
For when it might be needed?
Shall I be the sparkler in the cocktail
Spitting white-hot stars
And burning my words onto retinas
of many mind's eyes?
Or yet a single lonely candle
Lit to draw a lost soul home,
Set in window and left to flicker
Where few if any will see?
Put me then to the test:

Set a match to me,
Watch me burning
And see how long I last.

Coracle

Cast adrift, I float.
My boat a simple coracle:
Bent withies, rawhide shell,
No sail, no paddles.
Calm as a village pond
The sea holds me
Cupped in watery hands
I could step ashore,
Wet no more than knees,
Feel feet on shingle
And a heavy failure.
The current catches-
I whirl like lily leaf let loose.
Dizzied, I sit down,
Hug my knees and wait:
The farthest shore is near.

Dark Place

I am in the dark place;
So dark I cannot see the walls,
Only the light that glimmers
Faintly round the edges of my hands.
Not enough to see by,
Only enough to remind me
That I still exist at all.
I hear distant voices,
Too far off to tell
Whether they mock me,
Encourage me, torment me
Or are simply oblivious
That I am here alone
In the dark place again.
It's cold, but it always is here,
The steady unchanging chill
Of cellar or deep cave
Untouched by warmth of sun
Or the night-ice of frosts.
I am in the deep place,
So deep I cannot see the sky,
Only hear the birdsong
Far off in the distant world.
Not enough to climb towards,
Only enough to remind me
That the world exists at all.
My own voice rises,
Too indistinct for anyone to tell
Whether I am calling for help,

Or crying or simply singing,
Having forgotten the world out there
And have settled down to wait,
Here in the deep place alone.
It's damp here, but it always is,
With the constant moisture
Of rivers and the moving spirit
Untouched by the need to conform,
To twist the soul to safe shapes.
I am in the old place,
So old I feel like a child again,
Only the heartbeat of earth
Distantly drumming in my ears,
Not enough to dominate,
Only enough to remind me
That I am not truly alone:
When I lie waiting to be reborn,
I lie surrounded by bright spirits
Whose home is here
In the dark place,
The deep place,
The old place
And who wait to guide me
Back to the healing light.

Dark Waters

My own darkness rises to meet me:
As close as my own shadow and as dark.
No charm, no talisman, no prayer,
No kind words, no good intent,
No strong will, no firm purpose,
No amount of intellect or wit
Can even begin to save me.
Like a wall of water it rolls onward
Vast and unstoppable as the tides
That wash the shores each day.
The water fills my ears near to bursting
And I hold my breath as long as I can.
As I breathe out one final time,
Beyond the rushing waves that cover me
I'd swear I can hear whale-song.

Don't speak to me

Don't speak to me.
Outside the sun may shine
But inside me darkness reigns
And it must rule unbroken.
Don't talk to me.
It's not what's said,
It's the saying of it
That breaks the alchemy
Of thought and image and emotion
Brewing and bubbling
And transforming the shadows
That play along my walls.
Big or small, I don't want
To hear any words
But the ones in my head
Whispering beyond hearing
In the breath of the stones
And the voices of the unborn.
I don't want comfort
I signed up for war.

Dream Torment

Sleep, sleep, dive deep:
The Sea of undiscovered dreams appears.
Sleep, sleep, dig deep:
The underworld of hopes and fears.
Is it real or is it not?
Can I reach it? Better not!
Twists and turns; tunnels long.
A voice beyond: a siren's song.
Eyes are heavy; legs are weak,
Can I find the thing I seek?
Waking now, it fades away.
Forget it in the light of day.
At sleep-fall it comes again,
Lures me in, lets go and then,
Moves beyond where I can go,
I cannot run; I am too slow.
Dreams torment me, draw me deep:
I get no rest in nightly sleep.

Earthbound

Last night I dreamed that I could fly,
Take to the skies in a single stride,
Soaring above rooftops
Not like a bird but rather a kite.
This morning when I woke, I felt
Heavier than usual and burdened
By the gravity of my daily life
And bound to earth by boots of lead.
If there were a way whereby
My spirit might rise above the earth,
Leave behind my weighty flesh
And freely fly about the land,
What then? Would I leave behind
My earthbound life, tied by the merest thread
Of silver light, snapped or cut
By choice or chance to free my flight?
I sigh and know it cannot be;
I lack the skills to fly at will,
Except when I chance to know
My dreaming self and wake
Within the dream and leap feather-light,
Find my wings outstretched,
And for a time enjoy the skies
Until I slip into the dream once more.

Enough, already

Nothing is ever enough:
each mountain I climb
is part of a never-ending range
each one higher than the last
Nothing I do is ever quite right
there's always a flaw
that crushes the whole
and reduces it to rubble.
There's never a sense of the final
the perfect, the complete
There's always still more to do
More to polish and refine
To winnow and thresh
till there's nothing left
It's not like panning for gold
This incessant swishing and washing
where what remains is the real deal.
It washes the life out of things
It beats the vibrant newborn shine
to replace it with layers of lacquer
and French polish and wax
And the real rough hewn beauty is lost
Take a freshly birthed conker
Still moist from its casing
keep it and steep it
Rub it with vinegar
Pierce it with string
Let the contest begin
My money's on the new one.

Half light, half life

Half light, half life
Nothing complete,
Nothing finished,
Trapped.
Limbo-land lady
Stuck between
This place
And another.
Neither one thing
Nor the other.
A traveller stalled
Mid-journey,
Map lost
Memory gone,
Plans forgotten
Waiting.

Here Be Dragons!

The beaten path is very wide,
Trodden smooth by countless feet,
Wearing it deeply into the land,
And cutting a track through time.
I was content for many years,
Happy to follow where others led.
Then one day the path ran out,
Ended abruptly with a sign,
Rimmed in red, that ran:
"Warning! Here be dragons!"
I stood some time alert,
Watching for flames and wings,
And yet none came in sight.
I waited on, still unsure
Until a single step I took,
Passed into blank uncharted lands.
And still the dragons didn't fly,
Eager to devour my presumptuous soul.
A second step and then I found
My feet were on another path,
Thread-thin but strongly felt.
And then I knew beyond a doubt
What the warning sign had meant:
Beyond this point, you become
Those very dragons that we fear.

If I run

If I run, I must run fast
Cut away the weight of fear
Untangle the confused skeins
Strip down to bare and shaking flesh.
Breathe deep, breathe steady
And begin the run towards the void.
And if I leap I must leap far
Leave behind the heavy life
Wind up the ravaged thread
Start afresh with naked bones and soul
Breathe slow, breathe steady
And trust my clippèd wings to soar.

Internal, infernal

I'd like to live without
The invisible machines in my head:
The constantly ticking clock,
The dynamo that burns my midnight oil,
The tape recorder that memorises the words,
Etching them with acid on my soul,
The bullshit monitor that scrutinises
Each and every belief and assumption
And says, with a sneer, oh yeah?
Just who are you trying to kid?
It would be nice to live simply,
Without my own voice asking constantly,
Why, what, where, when, who, how,
How many? For how long? What colour?
The clock is the worst:
Counting down to zero hour,
Never telling me anything
But the passing of time and life.
If you take away these infernal machines,
What would be left?
Would the real me crouch in a corner,
Cowering in the stripped engine room,
Naked and dirty, pathetic and small?
Or is the real me the very machines
That are driving me crazy?
Tick, tick, tick, tick, tick, tick,
Whirr, clatter, whirr, clatter,
Pitter, patter, pitter, patter.
Are they footsteps I hear,

Creeping up on me?
Is there someone there,
Or am I really alone in here?

Just words

No one listens to me.
But then I have nothing to say
I have not said a thousand times before.
I'm dying for someone to hear
My silent screams
And offer help.
I'm searching for the words:
The right words
The magic words.
They're just words;
They hold no power
To save or damn me.
Just words: no more.

Like a cold wind

Like a cold wind on a summer's day
Raising a crop of goose-flesh;
Like a cloud across the sun's face
Turning the day into sudden twilight,
I feel the change inside me
And I wait to see if the cloud may pass.

Like the sudden silence before a storm,
The birds that cease to sing;
Like the eerie stillness of wild-life
Before the earth shakes and the sea flees,
I hear the roar of the angry waves
Rushing towards me to engulf the land.

Like the blank blink in the bully's eye
The second before he raises a fist;
Like the juddering engine before it stalls
Leaving you stranded at the lights,
It warns of worse to come
And teaches you how to duck.

When the fog comes floating in from the sea
It's time to sit down and wait
Turn on the lights, wrap up warm
Stay just where you are; do not fight.
For like fog, and darkness and the bully's wrath
This too, like all things, shall pass.

Like a Tree in November

One by one I will let my leaves fall
All those things that hide my true being:
The words, the smiles, the clothes
Those outward things even I think are me.
Each one detached and falling
Slowly like petals from the cherry tree,
Surrounding my feet, shifting in the breeze
Before settling to begin the slow transition
To mulch and worm food and raw earth.
Then I shall stand naked, stripped bare
Like a tree after November gales.
You will see my true shape unmasked
By pretty colours and shifting shapes
And the confusion of shimmering sunshine.
Then we will see who I might be,
Beneath this coat of many colours
These tales of a thousand nights
And my Scheherazade soul
Who would spin out yet another story
To keep you entertained and distracted
From the true business of staying alive,
Will be faced with the final question:
Who am I?

Madness beckoning

This way madness does not so much lie,
As recline, like a patient lover awaiting
The inevitable return of the fickle friend,
Knowing that you might not write or call
But you will return downcast and contrite
To the loving arms of one who understands.
Going mad might be like going home
After being long exiled by sanity.
It might be easier than this ceaseless vigil
That watches my thoughts, even idle ones,
And scans them for the wild signs
That presage lunacy, and with the sharp kind blade
Prunes them hard back, cutting away
All hint of disease in hopes that the root
Will put forth healthy growth and blooms
That would not disgrace a Chelsea show.
Not then the strange flowers that fill my dreams,
Weird colours and malformed heads
Nightmarish and compelling in their way
As a car crash or lightning in the night.
Maybe madness is the way for me
To cultivate the crazy blooms of unchained mind
And bring to light some single thought
Never seen before today.

Man of Straw

You were a man of straw,
Dressed in stolen rags
Lonely in a ploughed-up field
Bereft of all but crows.
I dressed you in a suit of clothes
Gave you shoes and voice,
A backbone made of wood
And a bravely painted face.
You took these gifts as your right;
Your cunning crow-like brain
Told you what they were worth
Beyond this vacant land.
One day you'll stand again
In some distant barren place
Fine clothes sold, shoes in holes
Backbone snapped by time
Left only with that crow-led mind
And disintegrating straw.
I gave you just the strength to stand
Not strength to run away.
You can travel a long, long way
With someone else's power
You cannot stand a single day
Without a beating heart.

Masquerade

When I was young I could not see
That there was any way to be
The real person I am inside.
It wouldn't do; I'd have to hide.
Now I see it is my task:
Imagine life without the mask,
To be each day as best I can
That real person I know I am.
This means in truth that I would be
Daily naked for all to see.
Like hermit crabs inside their shells
We each of us protect ourselves
The core inside remains the same
Hidden safe and free from shame.
Only lovers can bear to be
Exposed to each other, in honesty.

Mend me with gold

Mend me with gold
Fill my gaping cracks
With precious metals
And loving care.
Do not discard me
Now the years
Have worn me
From my first creation
Smooth and unblemished
Untouched by life.
See the damage
Not as disfigurement
But as radical sculpture
Of a work in progress.
See every chip,
Every dent, every frayed edge
As a stroke of genius,
Of ongoing art.

Mud and tears

After the snow: the rain.
After the rain: the flood.
After the flood: the mud.
Snow imprisons me
And I dread the thaw:
Tears, anger and the mud.
What a mess!
But the black Nile silt
Laid thick across the plain
Made Egypt once
An Empire's breadbasket.
Let then the ice melt:
Welcome the dancing torrents
And await the healing mud.

My kind of wisdom

Just because my kind of wisdom
Doesn't wear buckskin,
Isn't hung with feathers,
Isn't decorated with crystals
And isn't inscribed with runes and sigils,
It doesn't mean it isn't real.
Just because my kind of wisdom
Doesn't require mastering
An arcane language,
Higher mathematics
Or a degree in theology,
It doesn't mean it isn't deep.
Just because my kind of wisdom
Doesn't ask me to stand
On one leg for years,
Beat myself with whips,
And starve myself half to death,
It doesn't mean it hasn't cost.
Homespun, home-grown, home-made:
You know, from somewhere far off,
It might look as exotic as yours.

New lamps for old

New pain is shrill:
Screaming sirens and squealing tyres.
It thunders in the ears
Pulsing with passion,
Crimson coated across the retina:
The loud insistent throb
Of deafening music.
It hammers at your door,
Shrieking like a demented lover
Demanding your attention.

Old pain is quiet,
Lodged in bones and gut,
Buried in muscle
Hidden by fat.
A constant ache,
Dull but bearable.
A sudden scent, a forgotten face,
A careless chord and then,
Pain pounds, a brief flare
Of hot remembered hurt.

Night Shift
(for those who wait with the dying)

I want to hold back Death:
Impossible of course,
But every time I try,
Standing in the way,
Arms outstretched
As if to halt
A bolting horse,
It passes through
As if I, not it,
Were insubstantial mist.
And I feel a touch
Across my face
Of trailing cobwebs
Or frosted feathers
Stiff with ice.

Not again

Oh God, not again!
Haven't I done this enough yet?
Haven't I wrestled the midnight demons
Till my muscles ached?
Haven't I searched my soul
Like beaters at a shoot
Thrashing the bracken to death
To flush out a few birds?
Haven't I scoured my soul
Like a housewife with Vim
And a scrubbing brush
Spring cleaning her kitchen?
Haven't I lived long enough
In dark places craving a return to light,
A kind, certain word here
A signpost, an arrow there?
Haven't I done this thing,
This illness, this mad descent
Into a personal, private hell
Haven't I done this enough?
What more do you want of me?
Must you break me utterly,
Fracture the seams of my soul,
Unpick what stitches me together,
Crumble me into tiny pieces?
Haven't you finished with me yet?

Pain woke you

Pain woke you,
Prodded you from sleep.
From the first aches of discomfort
To the full blown agony of awareness
It stopped your slumber dead.
You tried to mask it
Tried to distract yourself
With whatever came to hand.
Anything to sleep again
Dreaming the soft safe dreams
That fill the sleeping world
With pastels colours and smooth shapes
And are void of any meaning.
So, the pain is gone,
You tell me without words
Life feels good, you say.
Sweet dreams, I say, resigned.
I'll see you in the morning;
I'll take the night-shift
And watch over your sleep.
Someone has to guard the sleepers,
It might as well be me.

Pain woke me,
Prodded me from sleep.
From the first aches of discomfort
To the full blown agony of awareness
It stopped my slumber dead.
I tried to mask it

Tried to distract myself
With whatever came to hand.
Anything to sleep again
Dreaming the soft safe dreams
That fill the sleeping world
With pastels colours and smooth shapes
And are void of any meaning.
So, the pain is gone,
I tell you without words
Life feels good, I say.
Sweet dreams, you say, resigned.
I'll see you in the morning;
You take the night-shift
And watch over my sleep.
Someone has to guard the sleepers,
It might as well be you.

Pain woke them,
Prodded them from sleep.
From the first aches of discomfort
To the full blown agony of awareness
It stopped their slumber dead.
They tried to mask it
Tried to distract themselves
With whatever came to hand.
Anything to sleep again
Dreaming the soft safe dreams
That fill the sleeping world
With pastels colours and smooth shapes

And are void of any meaning.
So, the pain is gone,
They tell me without words
Life feels good, they say.
Sweet dreams, I say, resigned.
I'll see you in the morning;
I'll take the night-shift
And watch over your sleep.
Someone has to guard the sleepers,
It might as well be me.

Patience

Mine is the house of ticking clocks
Discordantly measuring the drip of time,
Dust dancing in the slow sunlight
Of the eternal Sunday afternoon.
Time crawls by on rheumatic knees;
The sun rise, the sun sets.
A week of empty fullness passes
Between each morning and each night.
The seasons turn sluggishly round,
The surfaces gather dust to plough
Furrows in and sow the seeds
Of future lives and grime,
Awaiting the apocalypse of dusters.
Tiny kingdoms rise and fall,
Eternity in a pinch of dirt,
And I wait, patient as a stone,
For ripples of change to grow,
Circles widening endlessly in water
Altering without alteration
Until the world shall change or end.

Riddle

I'm a face in the crowd
The one you'd like to kiss
I'm a voice in the wilderness
The one you're gonna miss
I'm a fragrance on the air
The one you think you know
I'm a touch on your sleeve
But before you look, I go
I'm the one you've met before
But you can't recall my name
Like the heart in your body
I'm the one they'll never tame.

Shadow puppet

The shadows are there
Even when the sun shines
Even when there's a smile on my face
The shadows are there
Even when everything seems fine
Even when I can see nothing but light
The shadows speak in dusty voices
Soft as the ghosts of feathers
With spines of steel and bones of ice
Cutting to the heart of my dreams
They speak with poison and sugar
With a kindness that kills
The shadows are there
Taking the joy from me
Spoiling the daylight
Thunder clouds on a summer
Threatening me with war
I push them back with patient hands
To the deepest corner of my mind
And let them whisper their dreadful lies
I'll deal with them another time.

Sleepless in a hospital bed

My world has shrunk:
Bordered by weakness,
Walled with pain,
Curtained by wakefulness.
My world has shrunk
To this one bed,
This room, this ward;
My leash, an IV drip.
I'm anchored not by hope
But by stubbornness,
A sheer bloody-mindedness
That stops me escaping in sleep.
Determined to live
Each uncomfortable second
Each awkward moment,
Each pang of pain or fear
Holds me tight as arms.
I'm safe, I know;
My fears are fools
With louder voices
Than my common sense
Whispering of Occam's razor
And going home well again.
But the whispers are drowned
By the night noises of the ward:
The crying in the next room
Of a confused distressed old person
Going apparently unanswered;
The bleeps and clicks

Made by machines
Surrounding us-
And the traffic slowing
But never stopping.
I watch the curtains
Billow softly around me
In the night wind
Blowing warm from heaters
And finally let myself
Begin to drift
Into the safe, painless
Harbour of sleep

Snow Blindness
(March 23rd 2013)

It snowed again today;
I thought of you.
The fat white flakes
Like funeral feathers
of a car-crashed dove
Tumbled down relentlessly
And, as usual, I tried
To see each one.
Stupefied I stared, eyes
Glazing, becoming entranced
By the belief that each
Single lace mat was special
Needing my acute
undivided attention
And appreciation.
You loved snow.
You loved the way it covered
Each grimy workdays street
making the mundane magical
Or so you said.
Now I see that it was less
For the beauty but rather
For the confusion it wrought
On souls like mine.
Or for the concealment of filth
You'd rather no one saw.

Stale, mate

I'm stuck, trapped, boxed in.
Whichever way I move,
It brings me back to here,
Walled in and cornered.
I'm sick of the knife edge tango
This dance with balance
and the relentless Dark Queen
Chasing me across the board.
I tap-dance between squares,
Trying to escape with clever moves
returning always to this state.
Breathing space, for a short while
Means I can fool myself I am free
Before the shadow of the Queen
Falls long across the field
And in a few moves, I'm locked up
Pinned down and frantic.
I concede: you win.
No rematch, please.

Stillborn dream

Last night I dreamed I bore a babe,
Born twenty weeks too soon: and dead.
I grieved awake as much as if
I'd truly born a child that day.
The day went on, I soon forgot
The heat of loss, the chill of grief.
But underneath the wound was deep
And I'm still weeping in my sleep.

Strip cartoon

Take away my clothes
And what is left but flesh?
Pink and pale, shivering
Stretch-marks and scars,
Muscles poorly defined
Beneath layers of fat.
Take away my success,
And what is left but obscurity?
Another also-ran
Amid the hordes of hopefuls
Bunched in the mid-list
Left behind by the winners.
Take away my words
And what is left but silence?
Ringing like an ancient bell,
The absence and memory
Of sound and meaning
Fading to nothingness.
Take away my strength
And what is left but weakness?
A wasting of limbs and sinew,
A withering of vigour,
Thinning to feebleness
And the shame of dependence.
Take away my visions
And what is left but blindness?
The future fading to black
The hoped-for worlds
Unborn and uncreated

Dying in the mind-womb.
Take away my memories
And what is left but emptiness?
A person without past
A woman without precedents
Unanchored by time
Unplaced in the world.
If you take it all away,
What is left of me?
How deep must this stripping go
Before I become unadopted atoms
My identity and meaning
Blown to the four winds
Like summer dust when gales
Usher in the autumn cold?

Summer's End

I have seen the stars fall
Piercing the clouds
With brief bright flames
White-hot and evanescent.
I have watched the moon rise
Pared to a mouse-nibbled cheese
By sunlit, lazy days
Of parched grass and airless nights.
I have felt the dew form
Heavier than rain, breaking
Drowned cobwebs with
Swollen crystal drops.
I have breathed the night wind
Laden with day-lost scents
Waiting only for the chill
Of dark descending.
I have heard the dip and splash
And beak-full calls
Of kingfisher, sweet surprise,
Where none were known to be.
And I have smelled Autumn air,
Fungal and fruitful fragrant
Amid leaf litter and windfalls
And drowsy gorging wasps.

Swansong

They say a swan sings
Before it dies.
But like many myths
It is not true,
Except for those
Whose ears can hear
A silent tune,
A melody made by
The severing of all
Those chords that bind
Us all to earth.

Test to destruction

My mascara has not run,
But it seems to have gone.
I like to put things
Through their paces:
Test to destruction.
My heart has not broken
But it seems to have cracked.
I like to put things
Through their paces:
Test to destruction.
My faith is not destroyed,
But it's certainly frayed.
I like to put things
Through their paces:
Test to destruction.
My God is not tarnished,
But he seems to have vanished.
I like to put things
Through their paces:
Test to destruction.

The Cave

I am going into myself,
Into that dark safe place
Far back in the cold cave
Where the light doesn't reach.

I am going into myself
Where no one can hurt me
Where no one can reach me
And no one knows I am here.

I am going into myself:
To nurse my grievous wounds,
To contemplate my navel,
And to salve my hurt pride.

I am going into myself,
Not to heal my soul
But to try to hear it
And find what I should do.

I am going into myself
Into that dark safe place
That light seldom touches.
I may be some time.

The Comfort of Ashes

There's something clean about ashes;
Rubbish reduced to uniform powder.
No heaps of trash to hurt the eye,
No rotting corpse to hurt the heart.
Clean
Simple
Impermanent.
A gust of wind, a wash of water
And it's gone for good:
Dissolved
Dispersed
Disappeared.
It does not disturb me that I am such dust;
What the fire cannot touch
Never can be touched
By hand or flame or even eyes.
Let then the residual ash be blown
On the wind and be gone,
Returned to the kind earth
Whose bones gave me form
And let my soul go home unhindered.

The Dark Side of Love

Love has a dark face,
Beyond the softness
and sweetness and the lost days
Of cherished childhood,
Love has a dark face.
Loves says "NO!"
When we want her to say yes.
Love says, "Never!"
To our hopes and dreams.
Is this truly love then, who
Turns our love away?
Turns us on our heads?

The Exile

I am a stranger in a strange land:
The exiled, the dispossessed,
A refugee from life.
I want to go home,
Knowing it can never be,
That home is here, and now.
My mind walks alone
Through other rooms,
Other landscapes.
My inner eyes see
Other trees, other people.
At night I turn the wrong way,
Looking for rooms
I no longer possess.
As dusk falls, the walls
Move in, shrinking my cage
Until I feel trapped.
In sleep I escape to homes
I can never own again,
Exploring mansions beyond reach,
Castles and kingdoms
Created by dreams.
It's not that this life is so bad.
It just isn't mine, that's all.

The Road of Bones

There is a zone between here and there,
Where few would choose to tread.
The baking ground shines bright
With the teeth and bones
Of those who lost their way,
Wandered long without a map,
And starved and lonely lay down to die.
The clean white bones, picked bare
Of flesh by wily carrion birds,
Lie as their owners fell.
And if you can but bear to look,
To stare long at the path they make,
The way ahead comes clear.
My path is made of ancient bones,
Holding still their unspoken words,
Waiting for kind and patient hands
To lay their jumbled lives anew
And read the way their bodies made.
I cannot tell which way to go,
Which path to follow, where to roam.
Beneath my feet is only sand
That's made from bones returned to dust,
Gleaming silver under noonday sun.
No limbs stretch out, no fingers point,
No laughing skull grins at me;
Just pure white sand of powdered bone,
Stretched out till sky meets earth.
The sun is hot, the nights are ice,
But while the sand beneath my feet

Remains this eggshell textured sand,
Then I will know that others long ago
Have trod this road and lie here still,
Guiding my witless feet from harm.
The road of bones leads surely on
To what end I cannot guess;
Its end in sight, then I myself
Will lay my bones along the road,
To mark the way, while I go home,
On silver sand and joyful feet,
And leave the road of bones behind.

The Secret People

The Secret People are inside my head
The Secret People wait beside my bed
They wait until I fall asleep
Then climb right in and dig in deep
Their voices whisper the whole night long
They tell me stories, they'll sing their song
Yet when I wake and open my eyes
Their tales are just elaborate lies
Sound and fury and nothing more
And yet they thrill me to the core
Inspiring me to write their words
Before they fly like frightened birds
The Secret People are inside my mind
But the Secret People are never kind
They'll use me as their living tool
To write their stories and be their fool
Until one day I'll wake and see
The Secret People have fled from me

The Swordsmith

I'm angry.
More than that, I'm mad.
But the red cools fast
And I plunge the hot metal into water
Watch the steam rise
I look.
Needs more work
Back to the fire,
Pump the bellows
Watch the metal glow white hot
Lay it on the anvil
Beat the ringing steel
Till the forge sings
Again and again,
Folding hot metal
Beating it flat,
Shaping it.
Finally, the steam clears
And the sparks begin
Hold the metal to the grindstone
Hone it till the edge holds.
Fit the handle
Bind with damp rawhide
Heft the finished sword
Watch the light gleam
On newly minted death
I don't get mad
I get even.

The Tear-Glass

Dim blue-grey glass
Translucent still with iridescent sheen
A slender tube that once held
The tender tears of mourners.
Now long dry, the eyes that wept
And broken hearts are dust;
Even well-loved names are lost
As if written in the summer sands.
Yet, despite the years I seem to see
The ghostly gleam of newer tears
Still moist upon the fragile glass
And I must ask, as countless do:
Who will weep those tears for me?

(a tear-glass was a tiny vial of glass that was used at a Roman funeral in ancient times to collect the tears of the mourners and which was then sealed and placed in the tomb. I saw one for the first time today in a little local museum.)

The Wave

Damp air filled with the tang of salt.
The light is grey, dead, heavy with storm.
Wind rising, beating the water,
Driving spindrift to shore.
Gull feathers & seal bones
Litter the strand-line,
Tangled with leathery weeds
Stinking with rot and mussels.
I feel the wave before I see it;
A huge pressure on my aura
Rearing like a stallion
Maddened by lust and fear.
The sound, a hundred trains
Condensed into one deafening roar
When I see it, it's too late to run.
A mountain of water a mile high
breaks over my head
And I drown, crushed first
To a handful of pebbles
Rolling along the beach.

Three wishes

Every time I reach breaking point,
I find that I do not break.
Every time I reach the end of my tether,
I find that the tether is made of elastic.
Every time I think in pain I can't go on,
I find that somehow against the odds, I do.

Sometimes I wish that I might break,
Shattering into a million relieved fragments,
Sparkling like road-crash diamonds
Both beautiful and horrible at once.

I wish that when I feel that collar
Press and pull my aching throat,
That it would snap, burst asunder
And leave me sprawling on the ground.

And I wish more than anything,
That when I feel I can't possibly go on,
Tired and worn from trying too hard,
I might be given grace and space to stop.

Ties that bind

What are the ties that bind us?
Perhaps for some, like Marley's chains,
They are forged link by link
Of heavy frozen steel
To weigh down butterfly wings
And hearts that would be away,
As sure as nail through foot
Would anchor us to earth.
The ties that bind should rather be
Ribbony tassels tied to the rag-tree,
Love-knots given as fairings
To a beloved who will treasure
Each and every bright strand
Long after the satin strips
Have all faded and frayed.

Ties that Bind 2

Do not cut those ties
To those you have lost.
The blade hurts beyond bearing
And cuts more than you know.
Let those ties fray rather
In the winds of passing time.
Thread by thread
Strand by strand
Time wears the fabric down.
The first to fray is need;
Wiry like old roots,
It shrivels without feeding
Becoming dry and brittle
Before finally snapping
And becoming dust
That the wind catches
And blows away.
The next to go is illusion:
Flashing through rainbows
Of coloured pasts
That become slowly
Monochrome and clear.
You see things as they were
You see the truth
A skilful pen and ink sketch
Showing the bare lines
Of what there truly was.
Anger goes next,
Serpent-strong, writhing

Shrieking with fury
Dull red and thick with misery;
It grows quiet, finally
Stills its thrashing
Lies quiet and subdued.
You look again,
And it's gone.
Each strand that bound you
One by one wears out
Frays to nothing
Snap!
It's gone.
And when each tie is gone,
You may find that one alone remains,
Bright shining silver,
Gleaming in the kinder light
That time will bring you.
This is the thread that never frays
Never breaks, never snaps.
If at the end of all the threads
This one remains,
Then leave it be.
Cutting this one
Only cuts your heart.

Time is kind

Time is kind:
Each night it wipes
The whiteboard clean
Of teeming words
And painful, wounded songs.
Each day I fill
that empty space
with remembered tunes
and fading rose-petals
browning at the edges,
Their fragrance ebbing,
a scarce remembered thing
topped up by surreptitious squirts
Of artificial scent.
Each day, I rewrite the words
re-enact the scenes,
Aware(but oh-so-dimly)
that what I write is not
what occurred
but now the memory
Of a memory alone
And therefore corrupt and defiled.
Time is kind:
One day I will stand,
bereft but with relief
And be unable to recall
Those lost and keening words,
And that blank space
Will fill with new and better ones.

Tired to death

I'm running out of "up"
So I guess I'm going down
I really should have known:
A smile followed by a frown.
Nothing lasts forever
And my energy is gone
Never much to start with
But I guess I'll carry on.
There's nothing there to work with
But so much I need to do
It's hard to make the effort
And just to force it through.
All I can think of now
Is lying counting sheep
And deal with it all tomorrow
When I've had some decent sleep.

Two Takes On Death

When people die, however dear,
There is a small and shameful voice
That whispers in the secret midnight grief:
"Thank God!" and breathes relief.
When William died I did not howl
As once I'd thought I must,
But amid the dry and sterile pain I thought
That nothing worse might come to him.
We who are cursed with the two-edged gift
Can see all futures and all endings
And sigh when worsened pains are spared
And let our loved ones go in peace.
How different then the warrior kind
Who thought it shame to die in bed,
Preferred a gory, glorious death
While we murmur, "Poor Soul,
He slipped away in sleep, thank God!"

V

I don't have a life:
I exist in the corners
Of the lives of others
Kind enough to lend me space.
No, don't shake your head,
Protest and frown,
Condemning me for self-pity.
It's true: the words say it all:
Wife, daughter, friend, mother.
They define me by my
Relationships with others.
My name: a jumble of sounds
Meaning nothing in themselves,
A label by which to identify,
Quantify, stratify and forget:
Put me in my box
And hope I stay there.
Me, I reduce my name
To a single initial.
It takes up less space, less attention.
And maybe, just maybe
Beyond all names
I may shine, alone.

Waking

Somewhere inside
A clock goes "tick"
And I stagger
Up the shores of sleep
Draped in weeds
And shreds of dreams
To face the day
Blinking
Rubbing my eyes
And wondering:
Where have I been?

Warning

When I am bold I shall wear purple
With red satin undies that nobody sees
but make me feel a million dollars
in an inexplicable, sensual way
I shall say what I mean when I speak
and mean what I say, whatever the cost
I shall not waver in my conviction
that I have a right to be here
I shall leave my face unpainted if I want
And not feel bound by convention or habit
To alter my appearance in the slightest
If that is not how I wish to look.
I will wear flatties even if the style gurus say "No!"
because as a work in progress,
I am a being of perpetual motion
and no one can really run in heels.
I will try new things when I find them
even if they make me sick for a week
I will not follow the herd, but
I may accompany then sometimes
For observation and learning
because, you know, sometimes,
it's nice to be part of a group.
But sometimes, I am far from bold
and I seek to hide my colours amid the beige
and wear underwear the colour of old gum
and say nothing when I should say everything,
shudder at the thought of trying something new
and hide from those who may need me

because to be bold is also to be a target
and a soul gets tired of being hunted.
So I will start small and work towards
an everyday boldness that becomes
a solid purple beacon of light
By buying those red satin undies
for those days when I need to be bold
and daring, from the inside out.

Inspired by the poem "Warning!" by Jenny Joseph.

What am I worth?

What am I worth?
Five K a kidney?
A snip, if you'll pardon a pun.
Bargain bin good looks,
Reduced due to store damage
And some slight fading.
A cheap sense of humour,
Tending towards blackness
But not quite sick, not yet.
That must be worth a bit.
A Lucky Dip of hidden talents;
Go on, have a gamble.
Even I don't have a clue
What's hidden deep inside.
That bland tub of sawdust
May hold mysterious gifts
Awaiting your longer reach.
Go on, I dare you:
Make me an offer.
How much? You're joking!
No way, no sale, pal!
I'm worth more than that, I think.

Wild

I feel wild tonight.
I want to do the wild and terrible things
My own heart of darkness prompts.
I want to fly with the owls in the night sky,
Feel the rush of air, the cold dip and rise of flight,
Losing myself above rivers and fields
Lost in darkness below me.
I want to run with the Wild Hunt,
At the head of the hounds and with the deer.
I want to swim in dark waters that have depths
I can never reach but can die trying.
I want to spin with the autumn gales,
Blown like a leaf to God knows where.
I want to lie on the cold ground
And hear the heartbeat of the earth.
I want to leave my body behind
That hampers me, and the face I wear.
I want to be the stranger
Whom no one knows and everyone wants.
I want peace from the storm that rages inside me,
The tempest and the idiot told tale
That drives me.

Wood-smoke

Wood-smoke blowing in writhing sheets
beneath grey skies laden with impending rain
The ground gritty with fallen, gnarled acorns
And the outer shells of horse chestnut,
The shining conkers lying shyly among leaves
Fallen first from the laden boughs.
A smell of spice, illusory and fleeting
From the foliage turning slowly golden
Crisping slightly with autumn suns
Too brief to warm the earth much
Beyond the surface of the soil.
Birds tug at berries, peck at brambles
Seeking sweetness they cannot taste.
The rain comes at last, changing the scents
Filling the air with petrichor and promise.
We hunker down, collars turned
And make for home and hearth.

Will you hold my hand?

Will you hold my hand
As I sit in the darkness?
Will you sit with me,
Make darkness less lonely?
Will you give my hand
A gentle squeeze,
Warm my cold flesh
With warmer skin?

Please do not tell me
About a light I cannot see.
I will not believe you
And the dark will be denser
For the lies I think
You tell me then.
My eyes are wide open
And I am not blind.

Will you hear my words
As we sit the long night out
Without disputing my right
To voice my thoughts?
Will you let me speak
My soul's story aloud
Without interrupting
With unneeded reassurance?

Just take my hand
Sit with me in silence

Let the darkness be dark
And wait with me.

Afterword

This is my third collection of poetry to be published and I hope that you have enjoyed the poems. I began writing poetry as a small child, but by my teens I stopped. I came back to it as an adult in early middle age and found it gave voice to thoughts and feelings in a way that prose, my first love, simply could not. Poetry is a deeply unfashionable thing these days and calling oneself a poet is only liable to have people edge away from you. It's probably this that has meant it took so long before I started allowing my poetry to see the light of day on my blog, Zen and the Art of Tightrope Walking. Gone are the days of the poet-rockstars like Byron, but I can hope that my work reaches those few folks who still enjoy the art of enjoying poetry.

If you have enjoyed these poems, tell your friends and perhaps even write a review.

Also by Vivienne Tuffnell:

Poetry:
Accidental Emeralds - poems of longing
Hallowed Hollow – poems of doubt, faith and
exploration of both

Novels:
Away With The Fairies
Square Peg
The Bet
Strangers and Pilgrims

Short Stories:
The Wild Hunt and other Tales
The Moth's Kiss

Non-fiction:
Meditating with Aromatics
Depression and the Art Of Tightrope Walking

Printed in Great Britain
by Amazon

28865379R00050